Unanswered Prayer

Neville Stephens

ISBN: 978-1-78364-387-5

www.obt.org.uk

****

The Open Bible Trust
Fordland Mount, Upper Basildon, Reading, RG8 8LU, UK.

Contents

Introduction

Introduction

One of the most perplexing problems facing Christians today is why they do not see more answers to their prayers. Or to be more accurate, why they do not see more *positive* answers to their intercessions, for we know that the Lord answers *all* prayers. Sometimes the answer is "yes", often the reply is "no", though sometimes it can be "wait" or "not yet". All prayers, then, are answered although we understand the negative answers to be answers only by faith.

This, however, does not satisfy some Christians. They go to the Scriptures, God's infallible Word, and read such promises as:

- "If you have faith as small as a mustard seed, you can say to this mountain, 'Move from here to there' and it will move. Nothing will be impossible for you" (Matt.17:20);
- "I tell you that if two of you on earth agree about anything you ask for, it will be done

for you by My Father in heaven" (Matt. 18:19);

- "If you believe, you will receive whatever you ask for in prayer" (Matt. 21:22);
- "I will do whatever you ask in My name, so that the Son may bring glory to the Father. You may ask Me for anything in My name, and I will do it" (John 14:13,14);
- "I tell you the truth, My Father will give you whatever you ask in My name" (John 16:23).

Encouraged by such words from their Lord and Saviour, they pray fervently for the sick to be healed, for the local church to expand, for their family and loved-ones to grow – all requests which must surely be in accordance with the will of God. Yet when the answers they want do not materialize, they may begin to question the Lord, doubt His Word or even doubt their own faith.

It certainly cannot be the will of the Lord to have his children distressed because such prayers are not answered as they would wish, but neither does the Saviour contradict Himself nor go back on His promises. And He is certainly not the author of confusion. So what then is the problem and what is the solution?

It is the aim of this booklet to investigate what the New Testament authors have to say about intercessory prayer; to establish where they agree and where they differ; to see for what sort of events they encourage prayer; and to draw comparisons with our prayer lives today so that we can see where we are going wrong.

This last point is absolutely vital. If we are making requests and supplications in error, there is no way the Lord can answer the prayer other than with an emphatic "No". This is an important lesson for all to learn.

We have to determine what the will of the Lord is for us in today's society for it does appear to change from dispensation to dispensation and the Bible unfolds the purpose of the Almighty for His people. His character and nature never change but his dealings with His followers sometimes do. Some teachings are truth for all time and for all people whereas others may be only for a particular time period or a particular company of His children. We have to learn to distinguish these differences, and when we do so it will assist us greatly when we approach the throne of grace.

Chapter One: Prayers in the Gospels

Chapter One: Prayers in the Gospels

There are nearly a hundred references to prayer in the four Gospels, and in a booklet of this size it would be impossible to study each one in detail. In particular, it is the subject of intercessory prayer which we need to investigate for there are many other facets to this deep area of prayer. The enquiry being taken, however, is to establish why so few prayers today are answered in dynamic fashion, therefore we will concentrate our attention on some of the major claims and promises made by the Saviour.

Let us commence with the five references already quoted in the introduction. The first one is found in Matthew 17:20 where the Lord explains that mountains can be moved by faith and that "nothing will be impossible for you". Who are the "you"? Who was Christ speaking to? We need to note this, for the Lord was clearly talking to the twelve disciples (verse 19). He made this promise to them alone and no one else.

It is very easy for us to take a verse of Scripture out of its context and apply it to us today. This is a dangerous thing for us to do and an abuse of the Word of God. The disciples were given many privileges which have not been afforded us. For example, in Matthew 19:28 and Luke 22:30 they are told that they are to sit on twelve thrones, judging the twelve tribes of Israel. Some-thing promised to no-one else.

Moving on to the next chapter, we come across another of these tremendous promises made by the Lord Jesus Christ, "if two of you on earth agree about anything you ask for, it will be done for you by My father in heaven" (Matt. 18:19). Once again we must establish who the Lord is addressing, and once again it is abundantly clear from the opening verse of the chapter that the whole section is spoken to the disciples *alone*, and to no one else. We must be absolutely clear on this point. The twelve were given some unique privileges which no one else has been blessed with. They were to do greater works than Christ Himself (John 14:12), but no such promises have been given to us. Similarly, they were given a special ministry and special promises relating to them. This is why Matthew 18:19 was true of the twelve disciples nearly 2000 years ago but is not truth for us today.

Our third reference takes us to Matthew 21:22, "If you believe, you will receive whatever you ask for in prayer". Once again these words were addressed to the twelve disciples only and again in response to their questioning. On this occasion they were amazed how quickly the fig tree had withered, and the Lord used the situation symbolically to illustrate the lack of fruit being brought forth by the nation of Israel. The Messiah was in the midst of them with His twelve chosen ones. They were dis-playing their credentials with power and majesty but their lack of response brought the indictment, "May you never bear fruit again" (Matt. 21:19), a prophecy shortly to be fulfilled when the nation was set aside in unbelief.

This was not to be for approximately thirty five years, however, and while the Jews were still the chosen people evidential miracles and signs abounded, and this included wonderful, dynamic answers to prayer for certain people such as the disciples.

We have two further examples of this in John's Gospel, and they both come in that marvelous section between chapters fourteen and sixteen where the Lord comforts His twelve loyal followers with the words of wisdom, encouragement and exhortation. During this loving discourse, Christ informs them that "anyone who has faith in Me will do what I have been doing. He will do even greater things than these, because I am going to the Father. And I will do whatever you ask in My name, so that the Son may bring glory to the Father. You may ask me for anything in My name, and I will do it" (John 14:12-14).

What tremendous promises! The Lord even tells them that they will perform greater miracles than He Himself displayed! This at first seems to be an extravagant statement but when we remember the prophecy of Mark 16:17,18 we can see what the Saviour had in mind. There He told them, "And these signs will accompany those who believe: In My name they will drive out demons; they will speak in new tongues; they will pick up snakes with their hands; and when they drink deadly poison, it will not hurt them at all". The last three of these signs are not recorded as having been performed by the Lord, and there were others like Peter's shadow and Paul's handkerchief healing people, (Acts 5:15; 19:12). So it is certain from Scripture that the disciples did actually activate signs and wonders during their ministry not carried out by their Master.

Moving on to John 16:23,24 we find some more of this type of teaching, "My Father will give you whatever you ask in My name. Until now you have not asked for anything in My name. Ask and you will receive, and your joy will be complete". This also finds an echo in the third Gospel where the Lord told His disciples, "Ask and it will be given to you; seek and you will find, knock and the door will be opened to you.

For everyone who asks receives; he who seeks finds, and to him who knocks, the door will be opened" (Luke 11:9,10).

It is self-evident by scrutiny of all of these passages that these promises were given to the twelve disciples, and to them alone. The *everyone* of Luke 11:10 is not universal, embracing *everyone* in the world. Nor does it mean *every* Christian of all times. Predominantly it means "everyone of you disciples", although others, like Paul, may have shared in the promise. To claim them as truths given by the Lord for us today is to distort the Word of God. Such miracles were a necessity for the disciples as they undertook the second part of their ministry. "Jews demand miraculous signs and Greeks look for wisdom" (1 Cor. 1:22), therefore the apostles had to have such credentials to endorse their ministry.

The second stage of their commission was, in effect, just an extension of their earlier mission, namely to proclaim the nearness of the promised Messianic Kingdom but dependent on the nation of Israel turning back to God. The first part was to accompany the Messiah Himself as He manifested His presence to the people, and the second was with the authority of the Risen Christ.

This was because the Jew was not set aside in the plans of the Almighty at the Cross as many Christians believe today. The Lord prayed for their forgiveness because the Israelites crucified Him in ignorance (cp Luke 23:34 with Acts 3:17). Because of this, the nation was given a second opportunity of responding to Christ's Messiahship during the period covered by the book of the Acts of the Apostles, starting with Peter's sermon at Pentecost. The Apostle is clearly addressing his remarks to his countrymen as is evidenced by such statements as, "fellow Jews" (Acts 2:14), "men of Israel" (Acts 2:22), "all Israel" (Acts 2:36), and "men of Israel" (Acts 3:12). This was also Pentecost, a Jewish feast, and those present were all "Jews and converts to Judaism" (Acts 2:11).

No Gentile was present, and in fact the first Gentile to enter the picture during the Acts period does not arrive until chapter ten. Even then Peter did not want to visit Cornelius because he was a Gentile, which would have made the Apostle ceremonially unclean. This underlines the fact that the Jew was still very much to the fore, and not cut off in unbelief as some teach. This fact will play an important role when we consider the prayers of the disciples during this Acts period in our next chapter.

Returning to the Gospels, we find the account of the withered fig tree and the subsequent great promise of answered prayer repeated in Mark 11:20-25, otherwise there are no other passages which deal with what we might describe as supernatural answers to prayer. There are, however, several injunctions in the four Gospels which remain as truth for all time, such as "Ask the Lord to send out workers" (Matt. 9:38); "pray for those who persecute you" (Matt. 5:44); "watch and pray so that you will not fall into temptation" (Mark 14:38); "pray for those who mistreat you" (Luke 6:28); "lead us not into temptation, but deliver us from the evil one" (Matt. 6:13). We also see such inclusions as the humble prayer of confession from the poor tax collector which gained the Lord's approval (Luke 18:13,14), the Lord's exhortation to persevere in prayer (Luke 11:5-8 and 18:1-8), and if we follow the marvelous example of the Lord in prayer in John 17 we will pray for fellow believers (v 9), for unity amongst believers (vs. 11, 21, 22, 23), for protection from the world and the evil one (vs. 11, 12, 15), for the joy of the Lord to be present with us (v 13), for believers to be sanctified by the truth of the Word of God (v 17), for all those who will believe in Christ (v 20), and for the love of Christ to be present and manifested in believers (v 26).

There are also many other exhortations to worship, praise and thank the Lord in prayer, but we are dealing only with the intercessory side of prayer in this study. There are intercessions and supplications recorded in Scripture which remain as truth for all time. On the other hand, there appears to be much which is dispensational. By this we mean instruction given to a company of believers for a certain time period only, such as those given to the disciples in this chapter. An excellent guide to the things which differ is to look out for a particular theme throughout the Bible. If one can find reference to the topic under investigation in the Old Testament, the Gospels, the Acts of the Apostles, the general epistles, and the letters of Paul throughout his two-fold mission to the Jews and the Gentiles, one will be on safe ground to claim it as a truth for all time. If, however, a certain truth is found only in a particular grouping of Scriptures, beware! Investigate further, for the likelihood is that the issue concerned is a dispensational one and is applicable only for a certain administration or time period. We shall illustrate this more clearly a little later with some vivid examples.

Chapter Two: Prayers of the Acts Period

Chapter Two: Prayers of the Acts Period

Our new section takes us to the period covered by the book of the Acts of the Apostles, a program of approximately thirty five years following the Lord's resurrection and ascension. As discussed in the opening chapter, the Jew was still very much to the forefront in the plans and purpose of the Almighty, and we need constantly to remind ourselves of this fact as we pursue this study.

During this administration, fourteen epistles were inspired by the Holy Spirit – seven from the pen of the Apostle Paul (Galatians, 1 and 2 Thessalonians, 1 and 2 Corinthians, Hebrews and Romans), and a further seven split between Peter, John, James, and Jude. The number seven is significant in Scripture, and following the rejection of the nation of Israel at the end of this economy Paul is constrained of God to write another set of seven epistles, but we will consider these in due course.

Further proof that the Jew had not been removed from the scene at Calvary can be obtained by a diligent appraisal of the fourteen letters of the Acts period together with the Acts itself. The reader is encouraged to satisfy himself by undertaking this task, and to assist the enquiry we offer a few pointers.

The Jew still had priority over the Gentile as was the case during the Gospels (Rom. 1:16; 2:10). Because of this he would also suffer judgment first (Rom. 2:9) and during that dispensation miracles of judgment were in evidence as well as miracles of blessing (see Acts 5:1-10 re the death penalty on Ananias and Sapphira; Acts 12:21-23 re the striking down of Herod; Acts 13:6-11 re the judgment of blindness upon Elymas the sorcerer; 1 Cor. 11:30 re death and sickness for abuses at the Lord's Supper; 1 John 5:16 re the sin that leads to death which was in evidence during the Acts period). We do not have such instant intervention from the Lord today, and once again we are exhorted to search the Scriptures to establish truth for each dispensation.

James wrote his epistle to "the twelve tribes scattered among the nations" (1:1), the twelve tribes of Israel of the dispensation and not to "all God's people scattered all over the world" as the *Good News Bible* renders it. This is a paraphrase, an interpretation not a translation of the original manuscripts, and must be recognized as such otherwise confusion will ensue. Peter addressed his letters to the same company of believers and proceeds to list the regions where his countrymen had been scattered (1:1). Paul wrote a narrative which was clearly aimed at his fellow Jews because of the internal evidence, and this became known as "Hebrews". We will do well to let Scripture speak for itself and not attempt to incorporate Gentiles into such translations by "spiritualizing" the meaning of such passages.

Even Paul, the Apostle to the Gentiles, always went to the Jews first during the Acts because the Hebrew nation still had the pre-eminent role in the outworking of God's program of events. He "proclaimed the Word of God in the Jewish synagogues" (Acts 13:5): "On the Sabbath he entered the synagogue" (13:14); he "went *as usual* into the Jewish synagogue" (14:1), for "it was necessary that the Word of God should first have been spoken to you (Jews)" (Acts 13:46). While they were still useable of the Lord during the Acts administration, Paul always went to the Israelites first.

We have already mentioned that Cornelius was the first Gentile to be saved, and that not until chapter ten, several years into this Acts period. But have you ever thought that he is the *only* Gentile mentioned by name in the whole of Acts? The first and the last! And even then Peter, the great leader of the twelve, did not want to associate himself with a Gentile whom he deemed "unclean". The Acts of the Apostles is predominantly a Jewish book, an account of God's servants going to the nation of Israel and offering them the Kingdom of Heaven which they had previously rejected under the ministry of the Messiah. It was an extension of the previous ministry, and a second and final opportunity for the nation to repent. Therefore we must expect this book, and all of the epistles written during this time period, to have a very strong Hebrew flavor. This will include many supernatural events, for "Jews demand miraculous signs", and this will assist us greatly as we continue our exploration.

The prayers of John, James, Peter and Jude

We propose to omit the prayers of Paul from this section. The Apostle has much to say on this matter in his fourteen epistles and we will devote a whole chapter to each of his two groupings of seven writings. For the present we will concentrate our attention on four of the twelve disciples who were chosen to be the authors of the seven letters known as the general epistles.

Almost immediately we will notice a striking resemblance between some of the features governing the prayers of these four Apostles with the instructions given to them by the Saviour in

Matthew's Gospel. This is not surprising, for the twelve were sent only to the house of Israel as we saw earlier, and indeed Peter, James, and John were described as ministers of the circumcision (Gal. 2:7-10). It is an often overlooked fact that, with the sole exception of Cornelius, none of the twelve disciples are ever recorded as preaching to or visiting the Gentiles! Their stewardship was to the Hebrew race. Ministry to the Gentiles was designated to Paul, Barnabas, Timothy, Titus and other appointed leaders. Indeed, Christ Himself is called "a servant of the Jews" (NIV) or "minister of the circumcision" (Rom. 15:8 AV). His message too was only "to the lost sheep of Israel" (Matt.15:24), and not once during His ministry did He venture outside the borders of Palestine or make a concerted effort to include Gentiles in His preaching.

John

As the Apostles were continuing the ministry they started in the Gospels, we may expect to find similar sentiments regarding positive answers to prayer. Examples of this are, "Dear friends, if our hearts do not condemn us, we have confidence before God and receive from Him *anything* we ask" (1 John 3:21,22), and "if we ask *anything* according to His will, He hears us. And if we know that He hears us – whatever we ask – we know that *we have what we asked of Him"* (1 John 5:14,15). Thus John is echoing the words of the Saviour recorded in John 14:13 and 16:23.

The Apostle John had no doubts that positive, sincere prayer in accordance with the Lord's will would reap dramatic benefits. He had seen the blind receive their sight, the deaf hearing and the sick being healed. These were signs to the nation of Israel that their promised Kingdom was near as foretold by Isaiah the prophet (35:5,6). It was part of John's commission. Therefore, quite rightly, he prayed for such events and encouraged his listeners to emulate him.

Despite his powerful approach to prayer, John has little else to say about intercession outside these two references. In his Gospel he mentions prayer on just five occasions, and these are just recording the words of the Lord Jesus Christ in relation to how He prayed for His disciples (14:16; 16:26; 17:9,15,20). He has no words of advice of his own. It is the same when we move to his three epistles.

Whereas Paul opened and closed virtually every letter with prayerful greetings and requests, John is the complete opposite. He does pray for his dear friend Gaius in his third letter (v2), but other than this there is only one other reference to prayer in his seven chapters. It is found in 1 John 5:16, "If anyone sees his brother commit a sin that does not lead to death, he should pray and God will give him life. I refer to those whose sin does not lead to death. There is a sin that leads to death. I am not saying that he should pray about that."

The sin that leads to death was another Acts-period phenomenon, as was the anointing and gift of knowledge (1 John 2:20, 27; cp. Rom 15:14 and 1 Cor. 12:8). There were instant gifts of knowledge and wisdom from the Lord resulting in "you do not need anyone to teach you" (v27). This was in fulfilment of what the

Lord had promised them during His time on earth (see Matt. 10:16-20). On the other hand, there were instant judgments from the Almighty for certain sins, as was the case with Ananias and Sapphira, and John describes this as a sin that leads to death.

James

James, too, writes about supernatural events in his epistle because they were in vogue during this economy. He encourages his readers, "If any of you lacks wisdom, he should ask God, Who gives generously to all without finding fault, and it will be given to him" (1:5). Note the certainty – *It will be given.* Who were his readers? The twelve tribes of Israel scattered abroad. When was it written? Early in the Acts-period when the Hebrews were still the chosen vessel of the Lord, and this is simply asking the Lord to fulfil His promise of Luke 21:12-15.

The Jews expected to see signs and results. We have another instance where James writes, "Is any of you sick? He should call the elders of the church to pray over him and anoint him with oil in the name of the Lord. And the prayer offered in faith will make the sick person well, the Lord will raise him up" (5:14,15). A double emphasis here on what God *will* do. The Apostle goes on to say that "the prayer of a righteous man is powerful and effective" and then draws a parallel with Elijah, whose prayers were answered in a dynamic fashion by the Lord. But here in James it is clear that the sickness of the believer is caused by sin he has committed and he needs to confess it to be healed (verses 15,16). This is part of the judgment and blessings of the Acts period.

There were no punches being pulled here by James. The prayer *will* make the sick person well (not the anointing with oil), righteous prayers *are* powerful and effective; prayer *will* even change the elements, similar to moving mountains as discussed previously. James was not misleading his fellow Jews. This was the truth for that time. It is *not*, as we shall see, truth for today. The letter of James is addressed to Jews (1:1), and contains a strong Jewish flavor. If we read

Gentiles into this epistle and expect to apply all of this teaching to us, we will be disappointed.

This is a portion of God's Word, however, and "all Scripture is God-breathed and is useful for teaching, rebuking, correcting and training in righteousness, so that the man of God may be thoroughly equipped for every good work" (2 Tim. 3:16,17).

There is much in James which remains as truth for all time, such as "with the tongue we praise our Lord and Father" (3:9); "When you ask, you do not receive because you ask with wrong motives" (4:3); and "come near to God and He will come near to you" (4:8). Teaching like this flows through Scripture from Genesis to Revelation but supernatural answers to prayer on a regular basis do not. They are found only in correspondence to the Jew, and from men whose ministry was to the Jew – and even then on only a few occasions.

Peter

Peter wrote his two epistles during the same time period as John and James, and to the same people, and he alludes to judgments that abounded during that dispensation. But in the main he concentrates on encouraging good, practical Christianity among his readers, and avoids direct discussion on supernatural events.

The imminent return of Christ, a prominent feature of the Acts-period epistles, is quoted by the Apostle (1 Pet.4:5; 2 Pet.3:3,10) and because of this he urges his fellow Jews to "live holy and godly lives as you look forward to the day of God and speed its coming," and "make every effort to be found spotless, blameless and at peace with Him" (2 Pet.3:11,12,14).

His references to prayer are nearly all in the first letter. He opens with an exclamation of praise (1:3); he mentions how these Hebrews call on the Father in prayer (1:17); he exhorts all husbands to be considerate and respectful to their wives in order that nothing will hinder their prayers (3:7);

he quotes from Psalm 34 concerning the Lord listening to their prayers (3:12); he encourages them to be clear-minded and self-controlled so that they can pray (4:7) and he himself rejoices in prayer at the glory and power of God (4:11 and 5:10,11). All of these aspects of prayer sweep across all dispensational boundaries, and are just as applicable to us today as they were when they were written in the Acts period.

In his second epistle, however, Peter does allude to some of the supernatural events of the Acts period. He seems to be referring to the outward manifestation of power, the gift of knowledge, and great and precious promises; so that "through them you may participate in the divine nature and escape the corruption in the world caused by evil desires" (1:3,4). Although he does not expand on these great and precious promises, as his ministry overlapped that of John and James it more than likely includes the promise of instant, dynamic results to prayer.

He refers to power again later in the chapter when he explains, "We did not follow cleverly invented stories when we told you about the power and coming of our Lord Jesus Christ, but we were eyewitnesses of His majesty," then he proceeds to recount how he saw the Lord transfigured in glory (1:16-19). These miraculous events did not cease at the Cross, they continued throughout the Acts period. Peter himself was miraculously released from prison (Acts 12:3-19); it was Peter who struck down Ananias and Sapphira for being deceitful to the Holy Spirit (Acts 5:1-11); and he was instrumental in several healings, including the crippled beggar (Acts 3:1-10).

Returning to his second epistle, Peter refers to "false prophets … false teachers … destructive heresies … bringing swift destruction on themselves" (2:1,2), possibly an allusion to the sin that leads to death. And there is another reference to judgment of wrath where the Apostle warns all those who fornicate and seduce. He draws a parallel with Balaam, who was turned by a donkey, and warns of the consequences of these people with sinful desires (2:13-16). Such instant judgments occurred during the Gospels and they do not today with the Jew in unbelief, for this dispensation of grace does not permit such interventions.

The final reference to prayer in Peter's writings is the doxology at the end of his second epistle, "Grow in grace and knowledge of our Lord and Saviour Jesus Christ. To Him be glory both now and for ever, Amen" (3:18).

Jude

Jude's epistle near the end of the New Testament contains just 25 verses, so obviously he does not have too much to say about prayer. He follows Peter's line with warnings against sexual immorality, depravity and how the Lord destroys those who do not remain in the faith, and he also includes Balaam in his list of examples of God's judgment.

He concludes on a positive note, however, "But you, dear friends, build yourselves up in your most holy faith and pray in the Holy Spirit" (v20). Then he follows this with one of the finest doxologies in the Scripture, "To Him Who is able to keep you from falling and to present you before His glorious presence without fault and with great joy – to the only God our Saviour be glory, majesty, power and authority, through Jesus Christ our Lord, before all ages, now and for evermore, Amen" (vs24,25). What a marvelous way to conclude a letter.

Summary

Promises of instant, almost staggering responses to prayer are found in these general epistles. We find several references to definite, dynamic results to prayer but they all come from ministers of the Jews as they continue their commission to the Hebrew race. The Jews expected to see signs and wonders to confirm that Jesus was the Messiah, the son of God (John 20:30,31; Acts 2:22; Hebrews 2:4), and these evangelists provided the proof.

But even these great men of God did not enjoy one hundred percent success with their prayer requests. Everything they asked for did not come to fruition. Paul's pleas to have his thorn in his flesh removed were rejected despite his several requests (2 Cor. 12:18); Peter was released from prison in answer to the prayers of the faithful whereas James was not and suffered martyrdom (Acts 12:2); some demons were not cast out by the twelve because of their lack of prayer and fasting (Matt. 17:14-20); and on another occasion Paul and his companions wanted to preach in Bithynia but were refused permission by the Holy Spirit (Acts 16:6,7).

Even during the periods covered by the Gospels and the book of Acts, when supernatural answers were received to prayers made in accordance with the Lord's will, some answers were "No". This was a principle the Apostles had to learn, and it still applies very much to us today.

Chapter Three: The Prayers of Paul

Chapter Three:
The Prayers of Paul

We have already mentioned that the Apostle Paul was constrained by the Holy Spirit to write fourteen Scriptural epistles, split into two groups of seven. His first seven letters were Romans, 1 and 2 Corinthians, Galatians, 1 and 2 Thessalonians and Hebrews and he wrote those *before* the dispensational boundary of Acts 28:28 when his ministry took him to the Jew first, then the Gentile (Rom. 1:16; 2:9,10). His second set is comprised of Ephesians, Philippians, Colossians, 1 and 2 Timothy, Titus and Philemon and he was inspired to write these *after* Acts 28:28 when the nation of Israel was set aside by the Lord in unbelief. Here, "the dividing wall of hostility" between the Jew and the Gentile has been destroyed and the two have been made into one (Eph. 2:11-18).

In the first section we will devote our attention to the initial set of epistles. We will examine what Paul himself prayed for, and what he exhorted his readers to pray for. And we will pay particular attention to the supernatural elements in these letters, for it is important to remember that during the time he wrote these precious portions of Scripture, James and John were encouraging prayers of the miraculous type. Paul had every opportunity to do the same, as his readership would predominantly be Hebrews who still demanded signs as credentials. As we proceed, however, we will find *nothing* of the sort. All of Paul's writings are completely devoid of dynamic requests and results in prayer, and in fact many of his intercessions and exhortations include a very uncertain note.

Paul's first seven epistles

What we will notice from this group is the general rather than the specific nature of Paul's prayers. Into this category come prayers for other believers; prayers for their well-being; prayers for growth in grace; requests for prayer for himself and his fellow laborers in Christ; and exhortations to praise, worship and thank the

Lord in prayer. The reader is urged to satisfy himself by reading these Scriptures for himself, but these themes constantly occur and the following list might be of assistance:

Romans

Thanksgiving for the faith of the Romans (1:8); Paul constantly remembered them in his prayers (1:9); he prayed for opened doors to visit them (1:10); doxology of praise and worship (11:33-36); exhortation to be faithful in prayer (12:12); request to pray for Paul, his deliverance and his service for the Lord (15:30-32); closing doxology of worship (16:25-27).

1 Corinthians

Thanksgiving for the Corinthians (1:4); "Devote yourselves to prayer" (7:5); thanksgiving for food and drink (10:30,31); thanksgiving to God for victory in Christ (15:57).

2 Corinthians

Paul is helped by their prayers (1:9-11); Paul prays for their reconciliation to God (5:20); more thanksgiving (8:16 and 9:12-15); prayers that they will not do any wrong, continue in the truth and progress towards perfection (13:7-9).

1 Thessalonians

Thanksgiving and continued remembrance of these Thessalonians in Paul's prayers (1:2,3); more thanksgiving (2:13 and 3:9,10); "Pray continually, give thanks in all circumstances, for this is God's will" (5:17,18); "Brothers, pray for us" (5:25).

2 Thessalonians

Usual opening of thanksgiving (1:3,4); "We constantly pray for you" (1:11,12); further thanksgiving (2:13,14); requests for prayer that the Lord's message may spread rapidly (3:1,2).

Hebrews

Exhortations to approach God with confidence in prayer through Christ, the High Priest (4:14-16); a call to persevere and to draw near to God with a sincere heart (10:19-24) "Pray for us" (13:18,19).

Galatians

No mention of prayer whatsoever.

****

Other references to prayer in these seven epistles include the intercessory work of the Holy Spirit (Rom. 8:16-27); prayer for the nation of Israel that they would respond to their second call to repent during this Acts-period (Rom. 10:1-4); exhortations for women to have their heads covered when they pray in church (1 Cor. 11:4-17); giving of thanks at the Lord's Supper (1 Cor. 11:23-26); those with the gift of tongues are encouraged to pray for the gift of interpretation (1 Cor. 14:13-17); and there is just one occasion when Paul mentions prayer in connection with the Acts-period gift of healing. This occurs in 2 Cor. 12:7-9, and involved himself, not others! Paul asked the Lord three times to remove his thorn in the flesh, but the answer was "No!" Therefore, there is just one occasion where the Apostle sought the supernatural element in prayer in his first seven epistles, and it received a negative answer.

Even though Paul worked many mighty miracles and wrote about them, we should note the low-key approach to the miraculous in these prayers of Paul, the Apostle to the Gentiles, during this Acts-period. It stands in direct contrast to the prayers of James and John, and to the promises regarding prayer which the Lord Jesus Christ gave to the twelve disciples.

Paul's last seven epistles

As in the first set of letters, the Apostle continues to pray for the believers in the various assemblies, the prayers remain of a devotional and practical nature, and the supernatural element is conspicuous by its absence. A break-down of these seven post Acts 28 epistles in relation to prayer is given to assist our enquiry:

Ephesians

Constant prayer for these Ephesians (1:15,16); Paul prays for their wisdom, revelation and enlightenment (1:17-19); he states that through Christ they can approach God with freedom and confidence (3:12); he prays that they may be strengthened in their faith and rooted and established in love (3:14-19); he closes this section with a doxology of praise (3:20, 21); he urges thanksgiving to God for everything (5:20); he closes the epistle with exhortations to pray in the Spirit on all occasions, to be alert, to keep on praying for all believers, to pray for Paul, his ministry, and that he will declare it fearlessly (6:18-20).

Philippians

Usual opening of thanksgiving (1:3-6); he prays that their love, knowledge, discernment and righteousness will abound more and more (1:9-11); Paul thanks them for their prayers, stating they will lead to his deliverance (1:19,20); he pleads with them to rejoice in the Lord and to commit everything to Him in prayer with thanksgiving (4:4-6).

Colossians

Salutation of thanksgiving (1:3,4); constant prayers for these Colossians to bear good fruit, and grow in knowledge, strength, endurance, patience and joy, giving thanks to God (1:9-12); Paul exhorts them to do everything in the name of Christ, giving thanks to the Father (3:15-17); he tells them to devote themselves to prayer, to be watchful and thankful, to pray for him, pray for open doors for his message and pray that he may proclaim it clearly (4:2-4); and he closes with reference to Epaphras who was "always wrestling in prayer" for these Colossians (4:12) to confirm the importance of perseverance in prayer.

1 Timothy

Paul urges "prayers, intercessions and thanksgiving be made for everyone – for kings and all those in authority, that we may live peaceful and quiet lives in all godliness and holiness" (2:1,2); he asks for "men everywhere to lift up holy hands in prayer, without anger or disputing: (2:8); he states that all food and drink is to be received with thanksgiving because it is consecrated by prayer (4:4,5); he offers the example of the God-fearing widow who "continues night and day to pray and to ask God for help" (5:5); and he closes with another one of his doxologies of praise (6:12-16).

2 Timothy

Paul opens by stating that he prays constantly for Timothy (1:3), but this is the only direct reference to intercession in this epistle.

Titus

This letter has no references at all to prayer or intercession.

Philemon

Just two short mentions in this brief personal letter from Paul to Philemon – his usual opening of thanksgiving together with a prayer that he will be active in sharing his faith (vs. 4-6), and a closing remark that Paul hoped to be restored to his dear friend in answer to his prayers (v22).

It is also interesting to note the uncertain tone and the lack of definiteness in some of Paul's prayers in this section. It seems that the Apostle was fully aware of the change in stewardships, and because of the suspension of miracles and signs he was inspired by the Holy Spirit to adjust his prayers accordingly.

Illustrations of this are:

- when he prays that the Ephesians *may* receive the spirit of wisdom and revelation, in order that they *may* know God better (1:17);

- he prays that the Philippians' love *may* abound more and more in order that they *may* be able to discern what is best (1:9,10);

- and he prays that the Colossians *may* live a life worthy of the Lord and that they *may* please Him in every way (1:10).

These are just a few examples of the uncertain nature of the Apostle's intercessions and they stand in stark contrast to the positive, dynamic requests made by James and John. However, perhaps they are highlighted even more clearly in Paul's relation to illness.

- He prayed for Timothy, but because of his doubts of an instantaneous cure he encouraged his young friend to take some wine for his bodily complaints (1 Tim. 5:23);

- Paul had to leave Trophimus sick at Miletus because he could not heal him (2 Tim. 4:20);

- and he was not able to assist Epaphroditus who was ill and near to death, but thanked God that He had mercy on him (Phil. 2:25-27).

There was his own thorn in the flesh (2 Cor. 12:7), of course, and further confirmation that he did not expect the positive and dynamic answers to prayer previously proclaimed by James and John is established by the uncertainty of his return to Philippi and his sending Timothy in his place (Phil. 2:19-24).

Other than these references, Paul has little else to say on prayer, and even when giving instructions to Titus and Timothy on how to live their lives and how to conduct their churches, there is no directive concerning prayer. The Apostle lists qualifications regarding deacons and bishops, and instructions on how "to conduct themselves in God's household, which is the church of the living God" (1 Tim. 3:15), and he urges Timothy to "devote yourself to the public reading of Scripture, to preaching and to teaching: (4:13), but on the subject of prayer Paul seems to keep a low profile.

Intercession is important, of course, and there is no doubt that the Apostle commanded the constant use of prayer, but he does not lay any stress on the sensational or miraculous in this connection. In fact, it is quite the opposite, and his epistles are completely devoid of such requests before the throne of grace. Come with boldness and confidence, yes (Heb. 4:14-16) but do not make demands of the Lord expecting Him to fulfil them. This was the prerogative of James and John and those who were ministers to Israel during the Acts period.

Promises of miraculous responses to prayer are found in the Gospels and in the epistles of James and John, but when we progress to the writings of Paul we find no such sentiments. Even during his first seven pieces of correspondence, when the Jew was still in the pre-eminent role, Paul refrains from using such ecstatic language. The Apostle to the Gentiles never made the claims and promises of the ministers to the circumcision. If the Holy Spirit had wanted us to emulate the twelve disciples in relation to their prayer lives, He would have inspired Paul to include such commands in his epistles. He did not, and we must take as much notice of what is omitted from the instructions to the church, the Body of Christ, as we do of what is included. The Holy Spirit inspires deletions as well as additions, particularly when the stewardship or economy changes, and we will do well to take notice of such changes.

Chapter Four:
Basic principles which should govern our prayers today

Chapter Four:
Basic principles
which should govern
our prayers today

Before we approach the throne of grace and deliver our requests and petitions to the Lord, we need to realize that there are certain rules which should govern our prayer lives. We need to know why we should pray, how we should pray, how long should we pray, why we should persevere in prayer, then we can progress to the more difficult questions of what to pray for and whether or not we should look for positive dynamic answers to prayer.

Why should we pray?

If God is sovereign, and as the Alpha and Omega knows the end from the beginning, why should we pray at all? Do our prayers have any effect on

His plans and purposes? Even the Lord Jesus Himself said, "Your Father knows what you need before you ask Him: (Matt. 6:8) before teaching His disciples how to pray, therefore why make supplications if the Almighty is already aware of them? Job, in his despair, asked a similar question, "Who is the Almighty, that we should serve Him? What would we gain by praying to Him" (21:15).

The simple answer to these questions is that it is the Lord's will that we pray to Him. Ezekiel 35 records many things that the Lord said He was going to do for Israel yet, in verse 37, He states, "I will yet for this be enquired of by the house of Israel, to do it for them." The whole Bible is emphatic on this matter. David stated that "morning by morning, O Lord, you hear my voice; morning by morning I lay my requests before you and wait in expectation", and "Let everyone who is godly pray to you while you may be found: (Psalms 5:2; 32:6). Why? Because, "great is the Lord and most worthy of praise; His greatness no one can fathom: (Psalms 145:3, see also Psalms 18:3; 48:1; 96:4; 113:3).

In the New Testament Paul stated on no less than six occasions that he prayed without ceasing, or constantly (Rom. 1:9; 1 Thess. 1:3; 2:13; Eph. 1:16; Col; 1:9; 2 Tim. 2:8). Why? Because, "He is able to do immeasurably more than all we ask or imagine, according to His power that is at work within us" (Eph. 3:20). This is undoubtedly true but whether He chooses to do so, that is up to Him. He promised the disciples He would do it for them and in the Acts Period we see the record of His doing so, (e.g. James 5:16). For us living today, He has not been as definite but He can still use that power should He wish.

God is worthy of praise, worship and prayer. He, Who gives us life, health and an abundance of blessings wants us to thank and praise Him, two vital ingredients of prayer. He also wants us to ask Him for guidance and assistance, because as a loving Father He does not want to see us go astray. And He wants us to turn to Him in times of difficulty, because He is able to help us, and no father likes to see his children suffer. "Cast all your anxiety on Him because *he cares for you*" (1 Peter 5:7). He can take our burdens. They may be too heavy on occasions for us, but they are *never* too heavy for Him.

Why should we pray then? Because it is the will of God for us and it is a Scriptural command that runs throughout the Old Testament, the Gospels, the Acts period, the epistles of James and Peter and the letters of Paul on both sides of the Acts 28 dispensational boundary. When we can see so many texts, we can be absolutely certain that the doctrine in question is truth for all time, and not a dispensational item. The Almighty is worthy of our prayers and praise, and of course it is a tremendous privilege for us to have direct access to the Lord, and one we should not take lightly (Heb. 10:19-24 and 4:14-16).

How should we pray?

There is probably no better example of how to pray than that afforded us by the Lord Jesus Christ when the disciples asked Him this very same question. His model prayer offers a broad structure for us to follow. The Lord is to be first, and praise and thanksgiving should be offered to Him. We are to ask Him for guidance in ascertaining what His will is for the world around us. Then we can ask for ourselves regarding our daily needs, particularly in relation to our sins, the people we come into contact with, and temptation in general (Luke 11:1-4).

The account in Matt. 6:1-13 is given in more detail, and Christ here made some further helpful suggestions in this passage. Be alone. Get away from the hustle and bustle of the world. Be separated from the distractions of earth and be separated unto God by setting your minds on things above. Avoid empty repetition. In this manner it is pleasing to the Lord, firstly because He likes His child to have a private audience with Him as befits His majesty, and secondly it removes any doubts that the child is merely doing this act to please the on-lookers. If we pray only when our actions are being scrutinized by those around us, it is poor prayer indeed.

Notice in this passage the lack of instructions as to the pose we should take in prayer. There are those who insist that all Christians should kneel while in communion with the Almighty, thus displaying the reverence He deserves. There is certainly nothing wrong with this idea but it is worth pointing out that it is not a Scriptural injunction to do so. God looks upon the heart, not the external appearance. Is the heart bowed in worship, not the body? This is the criterion we must judge ourselves on. Certainly it would have been impossible for Paul to bow the knee every time he turned to the Lord, but his attitude was always one of humble submission.

How long should we pray?

This, too, is answered for us by Christ in this same section. "Do not keep on babbling like pagans, for they think they will be heard because of their many words. Do not be like them: (Matt. 6:7,8). Constant repetition of the same phraseology, however spiritual it may sound, gains no respect from the Lord.

Even the prayers in Scripture are very short. The "Lord's Prayer" takes less than a minute to recite and the two longest prayers in the New Testament take no longer then two to three minutes each (Eph. 1:15-23; 3:14-21). Short, positive but regular prayers seem to be the ideal if we take the Bible to be our yardstick. Christ spent the night in prayer on occasions, but nowhere is it recorded that we are to follow this example.

Communal prayer-meetings with a group all interceding for the same event or person also do not gain endorsement from the Scriptures. If they were effective, our hospitals would be empty and our churches would be full! And if prayers depended upon the number of times they were uttered, the "Kingdom come" from the Lord's model prayer would have arrived centuries ago.

The length of the prayer is not important. The sincerity is much more vital. Quality and quantity is the key, but even then there are other considerations to bear in mind.

Why should we persevere in prayer?

Perseverance is another command to be obeyed. It does not change in different administrations for it runs as a theme throughout the Bible, and it does seem to be one of the governing features of answered prayer. We have a very good illustration of this in parabolic form in Luke 18:1-8. The opening verse of this section informs us that Christ gave his disciples the teaching "to show them that they should always pray and not give up."

He proceeds to offer an account of how a certain judge relented in his decision because of the constant barrage of pleas from a widow denied justice. And His verdict is, "Listen to what the unjust judge says. And will not God bring about justice for His chosen ones, who cry out to Him day and night ...He will see that they get justice, and quickly." The author is aware that this parable has dispensational tendencies and is quoted by the Lord with His chosen nation of Israel primarily in mind. Yet the principle still applies, and is a doctrine in Scripture that persistent constant prayer is an essential part of a faithful Christian's service.

Paul prayed without ceasing as previously mentioned; Epaphras was "always wrestling in prayer: for the church at Colosse (Col. 4:12); the Apostle exhorted these Colossians to devote themselves to prayer (4:2); he instructed the Thessalonians to "pray continually" (5:17); and the Psalms are bristling with references to persevere in prayer (see 34:1; 37:4; 40:1; 55:17 for some examples). The occasional, sporadic prayer seems to count for little and persistence in intercession is a must if we are to please the Lord, and expect Him to answer accordingly.

What should we pray for?

We are told in Scripture to look for answers to prayer, and indeed expect to see results. But until we can establish exactly what we should be praying about we will fail to avoid the confusion and dis-appointment many Christians experience today.

Obviously all of our petitions must be in accordance with the Lord's will, and we must realize that His plans do change within different dispensations. Therefore, we need to establish God's will for us today in this age of grace, and not attempt to claim promises given by the Lord to other companies of His redeemed children in previous administrations.

If we do not understand this principle, we could be facing a real problem for it would appear that the Bible is inconsistent and that God goes back on His Word. This is un-thinkable, and the Scriptures reassure us that God cannot lie (Tit. 1:2; Heb. 6:18); He cannot deny Himself (2 Tim. 2:13); His holy character never changes (Heb. 6:17; Mal. 3:6); and His gifts and His call are irrevocable (Rom. 11:29). If the Lord has made staggering promises such as "Whatever we ask, we know that we have what we asked of Him" (1 John 5:15) to those who follow His will and guide-lines in prayer, what are we to make of it when the desired results do not come to fruition?

We need to determine who the Lord made such promises to, and in every case it was either the twelve disciples or other ministers to the Jews. Can we find such commands in the epistles written by Paul, the Apostle to the Gentiles, to the Church the Body of Christ? The answer is "No!"

Chapter Five:
Conclusion

Chapter Five: Conclusion

What can we say in concluding this fascinating but often confusing issue of prayer and of what to pray for? When it comes to interceding for people to be healed or miraculously touched in some way, Paul seems very definitely to steer clear of the subject. The other Apostles do not, and we need to satisfy ourselves of the differences in their approach, otherwise Scripture would appear to contradict itself.

The answer appears to be that Paul was the Apostle to the Gentiles, even though he went to the Jews first while they still had the opportunity to repent as a nation during the Acts-period. Scripture tells us that "Jews demand miraculous signs and Greeks look for wisdom" (1 Cor. 1:22), therefore Scripture written predominantly for the Jew contains the miraculous prayers whereas the Apostle to the Gentiles is constrained by the Holy Spirit to omit such usage of prayer.

It seems to be that James and John contain the big promises concerning prayer, and as ministers to the circumcision this is not surprising. References such as James 1:6; 5:13-18; 1 John 5:14,15 and 1 John 3:22 offering instant, sensational answers to prayer were written to the Jews during the period covered by the book of Acts when these promises applied and were being fulfilled. Such promises, however, ceased at Acts 28:25-28 when the nation of Israel was cut off in the Lord's plans and purposes as a temporary measure because of their unbelief, and they are not truths for today. Nor are the guarantees contained in the Gospels which we examined earlier (Matt. 17:20; 18:19; 21:22; John 14:14; 16:23). These were given to the twelve disciples and applied only as long as Israel was useable of the Lord.

Therefore, I would submit that we are not to pray for the miraculous supernatural events which surrounded Israel in the previous dispensation but rather follow the sort of practical, devotional approach adopted by the Apostle Paul. He encouraged his readers to emulate him and his way of life, and this would include his prayer life. What did he pray for? I suggest that if we pray for people and events listed here we will not be far from the will of the Lord regarding our intercessions:

a) For rulers and those in authority that we may live peaceful and godly lives (1 Tim. 2:1-4);

b) For fellow-believers – their well-being and growth in grace (Eph. 1:15-23; Col. 1:3-8; Phil. 1:3-6);

c) For knowledge of God's will through all spiritual wisdom and understanding, leading to good works (Col. 1:9,10);

d) For open doors for evangelists and ministers to proclaim the Word of God (Col. 4:3);

e) That we might stand firm in all the will of God (Col. 4:12);

f) For the spirit of wisdom and revelation that we might know Him better (Eph. 1:17)

g) We are to praise and thank God in prayer for all His many blessings (1 Tim. 4:3-5; Phil. 4:4-7);

h) We are to worship the Lord in prayer (Eph. 3:20,21; Rom. 11:33-36);

i) We are to pray for the strength to abstain from evil (2 Cor. 13:7);

j) We are encouraged to pray for more Christian workers (Matt. 9:38);

k) We can also pray for the sick and our own bodily infirmities, but note the Scriptural response regarding the uncertainty of this (2 Cor. 12:7-9; Phil. 2:25-27; 1 Tim. 5:23; 2 Tim 4:20).

We are also encouraged to pray without ceasing (1 Thess. 5:17), to persevere in prayer (Eph. 6:18), and to be watchful in prayer (Col. 4:2).

If we pray for this type of activity it is in accordance with the will of the Lord and we will not be disappointed at the response. If, however, we pray for our hospitals to be emptied, hold all-night prayer campaigns for revivals and mass conversions, or insist on the conversion of a particular individual, we are likely to meet with sadness and rejection, as they are not contained in the Scriptural exhortations from the Apostle Paul to his Gentile readership.

We must pray in conjunction with the rules laid down for us in the Scriptures, written for our benefit and growth in grace. It is incorrect to go to the Bible, take a verse out of context and apply the blanket promise therein to us. It may bear no relationship to the dispensation in which we live. Let us realize that God speaks to different companies of His redeemed at different times, with different instructions to be out-worked. Let us read "the address on the envelope." If the epistle is addressed to Hebrews: or to "The twelve tribes scattered among the nations": let Scripture speak for itself and expect the promises therein to apply to the Jews. Let us not confuse the dispensations.

If we remain within the confines of the teachings of the Apostle to the Gentiles we will not go far wrong, we will be honoring the Word of the Lord, and we will avoid the disappointment of so much "un-answered" prayer experienced by so many Christians today. Remember, all of our prayers are heard and we can pray to the Lord about *anything*. "Do not be anxious about *anything*, but in *everything*, by prayer and petition, with thanksgiving, present your requests to God. And the peace of God, which transcends all understanding, will guard your hearts and minds in Christ Jesus," (Philippians 4:6-7).

We can bring before Him all our cares and concerns, our worries and problems. However, Paul does not say that He will remove them or solve them. He does say that we shall have the peace of God guarding our hearts. So all our prayers are heard and answered by the Almighty, but He will answer in a positive fashion only if our intercessions are in accordance with His will for our lives and are in line with the rules and regulations laid down by Him for this particular administration in which we live. Let us take heart from this, and approach the throne of grace with renewed confidence praying "with all spiritual wisdom and under-standing ... in order that we may live a life worthy of the Lord and may please Him in every way; bearing fruit in every

good work, growing in the knowledge of God"
(Col. 1:9,10).

More on Prayer

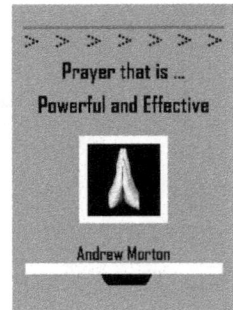

The Prayers of Ephesians
E W Bullinger

The Place of Prayer in an Age of Grace
Michael Penny

Prayer that is ... Powerful and Effective
Andrew Morton

Further details of these books can be seen on www.obt.org.uk

They can be ordered from that website.

They are available as eBooks from
Amazon and Apple and also as
KDP paperbacks from Amazon.

Also by Neville Stephens

The Twelve Disciples

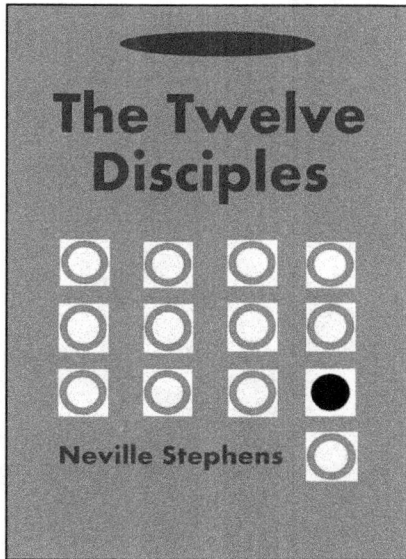

Further details of this book can be seen on www.obt.org.uk

It can be ordered from that website.

It is available as an eBook from Amazon and Apple and also as KDP paperbacks from Amazon.

Further Reading

Approaching the Bible

Michael Penny

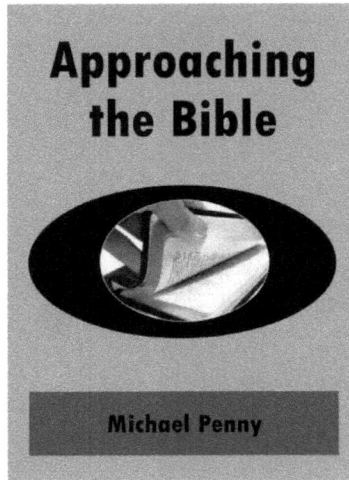

If you have enjoyed reading this publication on prayer you will find *Approaching the Bible* helpful and interesting. In an easy to read style and with an easy to understand method, it does an excellent job of following the advice of Bishop Miles Coverdale, which was contained in the first Bible printed in English. That advice was based on asking such questions as:

- "Who" were these words written to, or

"Who" were they about?

- "Where" is this to take place?
- "When" was it written or "When" is it about?
- "What", precisely, is said?
- "Why" did God say it, do it, or will do it?

After asking such questions, we then will have a better understanding of the passage we are considering and can better apply it to our lives today.

Further details of this book can be seen on www.obt.org.uk

It can be ordered from that website.

It is available as an eBook from Amazon and Apple and also as KDP paperbacks from Amazon.

Search magazine

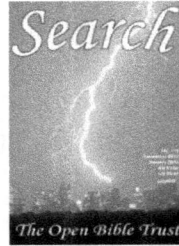

**For a free sample of
The Open Bible Trust's magazine
Search,
please visit**

www.obt.org.uk/search

or email

admin@obt.org.uk

About this book

Unanswered Prayer

One of the most perplexing problems facing Christians today is why they do not see more answers to their prayers or, to be more accurate, why they do not see more positive answers to their intercessions

In this publication Neville Stephens considers the prayers of the New Testament and comes to the conclusion that those of Peter, John, James and Jude and those contained in the Gospels' are very different from those of the Apostle Paul. His solution to *Unanswered Prayer* will be of interest and help to every Christian.

Publications of The Open Bible Trust must be in accordance with its evangelical, fundamental and dispensational basis. However, beyond this minimum, writers are free to express whatever beliefs they may have as their own understanding, provided that the aim in so doing is to further the object of The Open Bible Trust. A copy of the doctrinal basis is available at

www.obt.org.uk/doctrinal-basis

or from:

THE OPEN BIBLE TRUST
Fordland Mount, Upper Basildon,
Reading, RG8 8LU, UK

www.ingramcontent.com/pod-product-compliance
Lightning Source LLC
Chambersburg PA
CBHW070550030426
42337CB00016B/2439